STAGEMAD THEATRE COMPANY

DRESS YOU UP

A play by **WAYNE POWER**

Dress You Up
Copyright © Wayne Power, 2024
The author has asserted his moral rights

First published in Ireland, in 2024, under the imprint of
The Manuscript Publisher
ISBN: 978-1-911442-51-6
A CIP catalogue record for this book is available from the
National Library

Cover illustration by Cúan Cusack
Photographs by Alan Robinson

Typesetting, page design and layout, cover design by
DocumentsandManuscripts.com

Dress You Up

DEDICATION

for my sister, Aoife Power

ACKNOWLEDGMENTS

I would like to extend my heartfelt thanks to James Power of Stagemad Theatre Company, for fearlessly taking on this project and taking it to full production. My utmost gratitude for your direction and collaboration.

Dress You Up was conceived in 2022. I took it to Garter Lane's 'A Little Room' in May 2023. It was one of the most incredible and rewarding experiences of my life.

My sincere thanks to the original cast and to Joe Meagher and Ronan Fitzgibbon. We arrive at this full production with this finished script. It has been a labour of love to write these richly layered characters and see them jump off the page.

To Greta Rochford, Gerry Kane, Charlie Maher, Evie Burke and Jake Penkert. My warmest thanks for bringing these characters to life.

To Colm Kennedy at Bank Lane. I am extremely proud it will play host to this play.

To those involved in sound and lighting, costume and make up, thank you from the bottom of my heart.

To Conor Nolan of the Waterford Arts Office and the Waterford City and County Council for grant assistance.

To Ellenor and Jean Upton and staff at Waterford Centre of Music.

Dress You Up is dedicated to the underdogs in life and the queer community, a love letter to mothers, best friends, drag and Madonna – all of which, I am blessed to have in my life and am very grateful.

If this play inspires one thing in you, let it give you the courage to be brave and proud in a cruel world that likes to punch down and tell you to conform, to stay in your lane and hide in the dark, but to do the opposite.

For the millions of Bobby Burkes still learning to walk in heels before they can run.

Dress You Up will have its world premiere in Bank Lane, Waterford on Tuesday, 22 October 2024. It will run until Friday, 25 October.

WRITER'S NOTE

Thank you and let me all welcome you to the fantastic surroundings of Bank Lane and to *Dress You Up*. Come take a trip back to the summer of 1997 alongside Bobby Burke, his best friend, Mandy, brazen yet devoted aunt, Karen and his dad, Mick.

Girl Power is in, as is Fianna Fail, New Labour in the UK and we witness the final days of Diana, Princess of Wales.

I was 13 myself during that fateful summer and look back upon it with much love and reverence …and unbridled nostalgia.

My heartfelt thanks to James Power of Stagemad Theatre Company and to everyone who has played a part in bringing this production to the stage. I am indebted eternally to our amazing cast. I began writing *Dress You Up* in 2022, and it is a dream come true to have it make full production. I hope you enjoy this production.

This underdog tale is a celebration of colour and pride, of friendship and parenthood, individuality and courage, wrapped in grief, blasting Madonna from stereos, at a time when you would make your best friend a mixtape. Simpler days maybe, but with trials and prejudices that still endure in today's society. And of finding a way to stay true to yourself, whilst overcoming those same trials and prejudices.

Please enjoy this production and sit back and wrap yourself up in *Dress You Up*.

CAST

Charlie Maher	BOBBY BURKE
Greta Rochford	KAREN O'BRIEN
Gerry Kane	MICK BURKE
Evie Bourke	MANDY BROPHY
Decky Flynn	JAKE PENKERT
Lynda Gough	VOICE OF BERNIE FLYNN
Damien Tiernan	VOICE OF BARRY FROM CHAT

With special thanks to James Hayes, Dean Robinson,
Mary Power, Saoirse McCann, Woody Bennett

Contents

1. BOBBY – Opening Monologue

My mother used to always say to me, 'Be not nobody'. I miss me mam. She died last summer – August 1996. She was my idol really. Me dad said she was getting worse, but you don't ever think your mother is gonna leave you when you're 15.

Fifteen!!!! At 15 you're meant to be chasing girls. Shifting them. Drinking naggins in fields. Ducking school. I miss me mam.

I don't like girls. Well, only Mandy. She's me best mate. And me aunty, Karen. Me Aunty Karen bought me my first CD last summer, when mam took a turn. A turn. It's what they tell you when someone is about to die. She bought me into town. Karen always spoils me but I knew there was something up. She bought me my first single. *Wannabe* by the Spice Girls. Mandy thinks they're shit. Says they're all sluts and can't sing. So does me father. But they listen to depressing shite like Alanis Morrisette and Radiohead.

But I remember that day Karen took me into town. She kept sneaking sips of vodka out of her handbag. She took me to the cinema to see *Twister*. It was about hurricanes. Me father always said that Karen was the biggest hurricane in the town.

Mam's funeral was … I can't really remember it. Karen held my hand the whole way through the service. There was so much I still wanted to tell her. I love me Dad, but I can't really talk to him like I used to.

Karen and Mandy are the only people that know I don't like girls. I don't like to say the word. You know the word. It's what they call me in school. Decky Flynn is always calling me that. Mandy kicked him in the balls once. I think Mandy fancies him.

People just look at me funny. They look at me differently. Decky Flynn punched me last week. He said to me, mam would be turning in her grave if she knew I was a faggot. I told him to fuck off. And then he punched me.

Angie Burke. Devoted wife of Mick. Mother of
Bobby.

That's what it says on her headstone. I always visit her grave.

Dad nearly caught me one day – in me heels. I wanna be a drag queen. There's a talent show. I wanna do it!!

Mandy does the make up for me in her house. And I lip sync and mime to Madonna.

Dress You Up. That's the one I do it to. I feel like a different person. When I perform for Mandy and Karen, I'm not just the queer or the bender or whatever else Decky Flynn calls me. I'm actually someone.

I just need to walk in heels before I can run.

That's *The Immaculate Collection* – my favourite album. Sometimes, when I think about me mam, and when I think about what everyone calls me, I just put on me headphones. I cry for a little bit. Then it stops. Then I remember that I will be somebody someday.

And the world and Decky Flynn and his mother – they can kiss me stilettos.

Cos I'm Bobby Burke.

But I'm also Ciccone.

Diana Ciccone.

These are a bastard to walk in. But don't they look unreal?

And the world and Decky Flynn and his mother – they can kiss me stilettos.

2. MANDY – Opening Monologue

Bobby Burke wears stilettos. He's my best friend in the entire world.

Me and Bobby have been best friends since we were five: so, about ten years. I tried to shift him once. He ran off bawling. He's the nicest lad I've ever met. Most lads think I'm a slut. Decky Flynn told everyone I had sex with his brother in the industrial estate. It was 'heavy petting'. There's a pet shop called Heavy Petting. Bobby bought a guinea pig from there. He calls it Princess Diana.

He brought me to see *Evita* a few months ago. My god! It was some load of shite. Bobby beside me bawling throughout. And Madonna on some balcony singing about *Argen-fucking-tina*.

I kicked Decky Flynn in the balls for calling him that word. His mother, Bernie, wanted to report me for assault. She's a horrible bitch is Bernie Flynn. Do you know, she has a little grotto in her front garden? A grotto!!!!!!

I'm gonna egg it before the summer is out. And she has it lit up at night. She called me a tramp. I told her to fuck off. And when she was finished fucking off, to fuck off again.

Me and Karen want him to enter the talent show in August. His father will have a fit. But Bobby's really good. I do his make up and make him a few costumes. And he mimes to Madonna.

***

MANDY: Do you play anything else, other than Madonna?

BOBBY: SPICE GIRLS!!

MANDY: My god. You have awful taste in music, Bobby.

Why are gays obsessed with pop music?

BOBBY: Geez Mandy! Do you know many gays? Ya do?

Madonna is the Queen of Pop.

MANDY: She's a cow.

Bobby ...

BOBBY: I not turning it off, Mandy.

My bedroom, my rules.

MANDY: NO!!

You know Decky Flynn?

BOBBY: Do we have to talk about that prick?

MANDY: Look, I just wanted you to know I sticks up for you.

BOBBY: I know you do.

MANDY: In case you're thinking I let anything that dope says slide, I don't. He's an eejet.

I always stick up for you.

That's what mates do.

BOBBY: Sure, I'd be lost without you, Mandy.

MANDY: Now do me a favour.

You're blaring Madonna the past hour.

C'm'ere. I'll do your face and make sure it's washed off before your father comes home.

BOBBY: Awww! Unreal.

***

But Bobby doesn't know I've been having sex with Decky Flynn all summer. I feel like I've betrayed him.

But Decky is a prick. I do fancy him though. He's like a mix of Liam Gallagher and Robbie Williams. But without the personality. All I remember is him on top of me. And all I could see, in the corner, was a picture of his mother. Bernie and the girls on tour in Lourdes. Like she was eyeballing me.

You know, Madonna called her daughter Lourdes.

3. DECKY – A Fist is Louder than a Mouth

They never used to take me seriously in school, until I got to secondary school and I broke Mark O'Neill's nose with a hurley. Things changed after that. People looked at me with fear. Fear can get you whatever you want, if you use it well. Command and demand. And that's what I do. I command and demand respect. I got suspended for breaking his nose. My school reports say I'm prone to acts of violence. But I don't see it that way. I see it as acts of defiance.

My uncle, Frankie, taught me how to box. He won shitloads of medals and trophies for amateur boxing. They used to call him The Fist Flynn. He said to me once, 'A fist is louder than any mouth' and mine is quite loud.

Frankie doesn't box anymore. He gave it all up when he found God. I don't know where he found him. My father jokes that he found him on a high stool in his local. My mother is big into the God thing too. Fuck me, I do what I want when I want whilst I'm on this earth, and that's it. I couldn't give a fuck about religion. What an utter load of bollocks. My father agrees with me, but he's terrified of me mam. She lives up in that church.

And before I play any hurling match, she always rubs this St Christopher medal on me forehead and throws holy water on me hurley. Fat load of good it done me last week. We were down by six points. I'm corner forward and was all set to pull us back when their midfielder clipped me. I got up and tripped him, stomped on his stomach then lashed out at another two of their players. The ref sent me off. And of course, me mother. She stormed into the dressing room and gave me a bollicking in front of all the lads. And then me father gave me some shite about how one of his Fianna Fáil mates was in the crowd watching. Like, I'm meant to give a fuck.

I went out that night and got pissed with the lads. We always get into niteclubs. They know us as the hurling lads. I got with Roisin Dwyer that night. Fancied her for ages. There's a skip up near the GAA club. I don't really remember. She asked me to ring her during the week. I didn't. Why would I want to be ringing any woman??

I love winding up Bobby Burke. He's this queer in my school.

He hangs around with Mandy Brophy. I like Mandy. She's tough out, takes no shit. I like that. Don't know why she goes around with Lily Savage though.

He passed up the road one Saturday, when we were having a kickabout. There's a lot to be said for winding people up. Its fun. I like winding him up. And I don't like gays. Sure, why would anyone? It's disgusting. It's not normal, is it? Two men?

I see him poncing up the road. I kick the football over at him. I mean, I thought I was being friendly. I gave a right whack on his head with the ball. He went down like a feather. And then he tried giving me lip. Oh yeah, the mouse did roar. But I step on mice. And you know what? I admit, I absolutely loved him answering me back. I lived for it.

***

DECKY: Well go on then.

Get us me ball back.

BOBBY: Get it your fucking self.

Decky picks up shirt off the ground

DECKY: You'll be like a bent cowboy going around in that.

Did your alco aunty buy you that?

Is she like you as well? Some waste if she is, lads. Big tits on her.

I'd say you never saw one in your life.

BOBBY: Just leave us alone, Decky; will ya?

DECKY: Gimme back me ball, dickhead!

Bobby swats ball across stage

BOBBY: There's your fucking ball.

***

When I got home, Mam was in one of her moods. Made me go to my bedroom whilst she made another of her long-winded phone calls. She's always on that phone when she's in one of her moods. I could see she was fit to kill someone. Well, I wasn't sitting in. I was gonna go meet the lads and see if any girls were around.

When I snuck out, I could hear mam going ballistic down the phone:

> *'I know it. I just know it. Tony is meeting that whore
> again.'*

Tony is my dad. A few years ago, there was a rumour that my father was having an affair.

All I was told was that it was just rumours, started by someone who didn't like me parents.

But I do remember one night, being upstairs and hearing shouting and roaring downstairs. Me Uncle Frank was involved and all. I just remember me father walking out of the house, holding his hand up to his nose. Blood everywhere. And then hopping into the car.

And when I snuck onto the landing, I could see me Mam sitting in the kitchen crying, with a large glass of wine. And me uncle wrapping her hand in ice.

He just kept muttering.

'I'm saying it to you years, Bernie, a fist is louder than any mouth.'

I sometimes think it was on that night that me Uncle Frankie found God.

4. MICK – My Only Son

Everything changed when Bobby was born. It was like my youth had flashed by in the blink of an eye. You're making grand plans. Houses and holidays. Plans. Me and Angie wanted a child. I just assumed fatherhood was a natural part of life: love and marriage, wife and kids, nine to five. That, to me, was the circle of life. And I was happy with that. And yeah, they say life happens when you're making plans. And everything changed when I cut his umbilical cord. And he screaming the place down. He had such a shrill, piercing cry on him. He'd wake the dead. I remember the night he was born. It rained for hours and hours. The most dirty, miserable, typically Irish November day. The clocks had only gone back the weekend beforehand. I never liked the winter. I still don't. I feel heavier during the winter months. Everything feels heavier. I get down in meself at times. I don't know what it is about the dark nights, but they creep up on you. They swallow you, until you're counting the days till you get the first flicker of the grand stretch in the evening.

The night he was born, I was on top of the world. Angie was home a few days later. I got him a Man United baby bib. And I had a mini hurley made for him. And his big eyes looking up at me in the cot. You'd do anything for your child in those moments; wouldn't you?

He was a quiet child. I tried to get him into the soccer but God love him, he couldn't kick a pebble let alone a football. Angie told me to leave him be. The hurling went slightly better. Well, I thought so anyway. Bobby was well able to pull on a fella. He gave a fella an awful whack on the shin in an under-10 game. He got sent off. He started crying on the pitch. He took off his helmet and threw it at Karen. I was weirdly proud of him for getting sent off. I was. And by Christ, he gave yer man some wallop with the hurley.

When he was born, I dunno, I had all these hopes for him. I wanted him on the soccer team. On the hurling team. I wanted him meeting girls once he got to that age. Go to college. He's smart enough. He's no fool; that's for sure. But that's more Angie's side of the family. Although the genes escaped that Karen. His Leaving is next year. And there's a bit put away if he wants to go to college.

Is it wrong that you want to map out your only child's life, or is it just pure, unfiltered, unconditional love?

Angie wanted him to go to a stage school, but we didn't have the money. Bobby is well able to sing. That's my family you see. They used to call me grandfather Dicky Sinatra. He had a cock eye. So they'd call him Ol Cock Eye instead of Ol Blue Eyes.

And Karen tries to sing. She sounds like someone getting a prostate exam off Captain Hook. Fuck me, she's brutal. Karaoke Karen. Every Thursday night, she's up in Murty's with Rocky O'Neill – a little bald fella with a ginger goatee. A creepy looking bastard. Stares at the women. One night, she croaked the life out of *I Will Always Love You* by Whitney Houston. And she'd point at that little creep and she'd go, "This is for my bodyguard."

Bodyguard?? He could do with a box of Right Guard.

Angie would be choking with the laughing.

But Bobby, he can hold a tune. Too shy though. Too quiet. I wish he mixed with the lads more. He's mates with Mandy all his life. I thought they might be up to something together. But she'd run rings around Bobby. I leave the two of them up in his bedroom, listening to CDs. Angie killed me one night for trying to listen up against the door. I tried to give him the talk.

I'm a widower. I hate that word.

Widower.

It's as cold and brutal as the winter nights.

5. KAREN – I Drink to Forget

Angie went quick. They always say that, don't they, when someone dies? Like there's meant to be a certain speed to death. Angie was the best in the world. Poor Bobby. I'd kill for that lad. Absolutely kill. Me godchild. He's like me. Mick hates when I say that, but he is. He's got my ways. But he's still a kid. They think they have it figured out but little do they know. Sure, look at me. I still know fuck all. But I know Bobby will make something of his life, unlike me.

Mick calls me a waster. I don't know; maybe I am. I change jobs as many times as I change men. And yeah, I drink like a fish. And I ride all around me. But that's me. What of it? Sure, isn't everything about sex?

I love Mick. He worshipped the ground Angie walked on. Together since they were 14. He's a great father to Bobby. I can't wrong him. But he's hiding in that factory since Angie died. Taking every damn shift he can get. Sure, that his way of coping. Whet's mine? Alcohol. So sue me. I drink. I never used to. No, I lie, I've always drank. It's gotten worse since Angie was diagnosed.

Jesus, I miss her! Mick is always giving out these days. We both want the best for Bobby. Mick hasn't a clue. About Bobby being, you know, gay. I have loads of gay friends. I love gay men. They're loyal. And they smell nice. There's a few I'd love to turn.

The difference between me and Mick – and by Christ, there's a million and one. Mick bought Bobby a Manchester United jersey. And I bought him a pair of high heels from the shoe club.

I know all about what's going on in that school. I've been in so many times.

I know they're kids. But its always the kids that are different. I don't see Bobby as different. I think he's amazing. He wants to be a drag queen. And he will. I know he will.

We do what we do to get by, and I'm getting by. Just about.

People like to judge. They judge me: the wino with the loose elastic around her knickers. Oh, I hear what they say. When Bobby answers back, they hit him. Like Decky Flynn. And don't start me on his mother. I've had more run-ins with her. Big, bad Bernie and her duck's arse. She thinks she should be made a saint cos she gives out Communion in the church. I'll ram the Child of Prague up her fat arse one of these days.

And I drink. I drink to forget. I drink to remember.

6. BOBBY – Me, Myself and Madonna

Why Madonna??? Why not Madonna!! She's a genius. A visionary. Madonna is everything. I don't trust people who say they don't like Madonna. What's not to like?

My earliest memory of Madonna Louise Ciccone? It was *Dress You Up*. I just remember how her stuff was so joyful and carefree. The bubble-gum in her mouth, the beauty mark, the bangles and bracelets. The attitude. The songs. The music. There was a freedom to it all. There still is. There always will be.

And then I saw the *True Blue* video. And that was it. Smitten. My mam had that album on vinyl, on cassette, on CD. That was how to be a star. That was a blueprint in how to conquer the world. I was five living through that era: *Live To Tell, Papa Don't Preach, La Isla Bonita, Open Your Heart, True Blue*. That was how you did it. And to think, there was bigger to come. But my god, that era!

One night, when mam and dad were out and Karen was babysitting, she let me stay up and watch *In Bed with Madonna*. It was all behind the scenes on her tour. Did ya know, they were gonna arrest her in Canada, cos she wanted to pretend she was playing with herself on a bed on stage. Karen said she was a gas bitch. There's a part in it where she visits her mother's grave. And she just lies there beside the headstone. They had *Promise to Try* playing. I visited my mother's grave before school one morning. When I knew no one would be around. And I actually laid down at her headstone with my Walkman on, playing *Promise to Try* from *Like a Prayer.* I told Mandy. She said I should be sectioned. Then we both cracked up laughing.

That music. I wrap myself in it. I escape with my Walkman. Escape it all. I picture myself on stage. Lip syncing to *Vogue*. Doing the choreography.

I have it down to an art. I do *Papa Don't Preach* for Mandy. Her mother works in a warehouse that makes wigs. Honest to God. She got me a near identical wig.

I stuck a pillow up me tee shirt and put on Karen's leather jacket. And a bit of make-up. Sure, why not? It's only a bitta slap. For the laugh, I'd sometimes stick a water balloon up there and let it burst, like I've broke me waters. I'm mad like that, ya see. I'd love to do that on stage some time. Some time.

Madonna. The Material Girl. The Queen of Pop. Queen of the World. They hate her now. Cos of the *SEX* book. You'd swear she released *The Satanic Verses*. A few pictures of her tits and she's nailed to the cross. The cross she burned in 1989 in the *Like a Prayer* video.

I could listen to her for hours. And I do.

> *'Life is a mystery. Everyone must stand alone. I hear*
> *you call my name, and it feels like home.'*

That's art. That's poetry.

Sylvia Yeats couldn't write that.

7. MANDY – For the Love of Decky Flynn

When Bobby told me he was gay, he was about 14. Like I guessed. He's me best friend. I couldn't care less. We were doing truth or dare in my house at Halloween. He was dressed up as Gabrielle. You know, the singer. He had an eye patch he took off a pirates set he found in the pound shop. I was Sinead O'Connor. I had a swimming cap over me hair to make it look like I was bald. Me mother wouldn't let me go out holding a picture of Pope John Paul. So I took one of Gay Byrne instead.

When we were playing truth or dare and he told me he was gay, we both started laughing for a bit.

I have a crush on Decky Flynn. I go weak for GAA shorts. But he has no personality. And the little he has is repulsive. I shifted him one night. He's a good kisser, to be fair.

Decky wasn't me first. First time was when I was 14. It was awful. In Dave Kavanagh's shed. He didn't know what he was doing. Me, bare arsed, up against a load of briquettes. Decky knew what he was doing. And then he'd discard you soon as we were done. I know he was using me. And I know I could do better. And the guilt about Bobby felt its most intense when Decky would say something about him. I always defended him.

> *'Why you always at Bobby Burke? Do you fancy him
> yourself; do you? Something you want to tell me,
> Decky?"*

Oh, he didn't like that. But Decky knew I was well able for him. And I think that's why he liked me.

We only did it once. But we'd mess around the odd time. And I wanted to. My virginity wasn't some sacred locket that I was gonna keep stored in a box. It's just sex. Everyone has sex. They don't all ride the fella whose bullying your best friend. But who's perfect? I'm not. And yeah, I did fall for him. A little bit. There's always one; isn't there? I'd listen to *Fade into You* by Mazzy Star after he'd sneak me home.

You can't help who you fall for.

He had a free house one afternoon. His father was out canvassing for Fianna Fáil. And Bernie was getting her hair done. In a place called Turning Heads. The only thing she turns is stomachs.

I keep looking at mine. Imagining how big its gonna get. I feel like that film, *Rosemary's Baby*.

I haven't told anyone.

I'm not keeping it. Not a hope.

8. DECKY – Be Queer Now

I had war with the minor coach. He's a narky old fucker. Oh, he stood there and gave me a bollicking:

'You've been seen. Drinking in pubs and smoking
hash in the fields.'

'And so what if I have,' I said. 'I'm 16. It's the summer. You think I'm gonna live in the church, like me mother?'

'Oh, I'm sure Bernie would love to know what's
going on with you.'

I froze. My mother would kill me. And I mean kill me. She rules the roost. And this fucker knows it.

'You tell me mother and I'm gone from that team.'

'I beg your pardon,' he says.

'You tell my mother and I'm gone from that team. I
wouldn't mind. Yee'd win fuck all if it wasn't for me.'

'I tell ya something, Decky Flynn. You're gone full of
yourself since you got on the County team. Full of
yourself.'

'And you're full of shit.'

I rang Mandy Brophy. I like Mandy Brophy. I was seeing her on and off. Alongside a few other girls. But I prefer Mandy. She has something to say for herself. A lot of it, I didn't like. But at least she had something to say. Most of the girls I was ever with just wanted to be seen with me. They never said much. And sometimes I liked that.

But Mandy was different. She kicked me in the balls once. For saying something to Bobby Burke. I don't get why she hangs around with him.

The first time I shifted her. It was after she confronted me in the GAA club. About Bobby Burke. I punched him in the stomach, on the sly, in the school corridor.

She was going bananas. She went to throw a punch at me and all. I followed her outside and she calmed down. I gave her a light. And we just started talking about music. And next thing, I was shifting her against the wall.

She pushed away after about ten minutes. Ran off to meet Bobby.

On Wednesday, August 20th it was – the eve of the night we were all waiting for. Oasis were due to release their new album, *Be Here Now*. I'm in an Oasis tribute band called Slide Away. We're entering the ChatFM talent show. I reckon we'll storm it. We're practicing most nights of the week.

I was hoping Mandy would camp out with us. But she thinks Oasis are shite. She listens to Alanis Morissette and Radiohead. No wonder she's so angry.

We jumped the queue. I threatened some fella to move and he moved. Me and the band brought down a rake of cans. Sure, that's what you do. Rock 'n' Roll.

It got to 2am and we spotted Bobby Burke's aunty staggering up the town with some fella. His hand welded to her arse.

"Bobby Burke is a faggot," I roared at her. She was too drunk to notice.

I was half drunk meself.

We then rang Bobby Burke's house. I robbed the number out of Mandy's make up bag when she was up in my house.

We rang the house phone. He answered. It was him. I'd know his voice anywhere.

We all shouted down the phone.

And then I grabbed the phone in the phone box and roared, "If you walk into that talent show dressed as a fucking poof, you won't be walking back out. You'll be leaving in an ambulance."

9. BOBBY – The Wrath of Decky Flynn

I was in town on Saturday. Dad had given me 20 pound and Karen had thrown me another 20, cos she won the karaoke again. I meet Mandy in town. Mandy was doing her usual giving out about the town –

"There's fuck all in this town," she'd say.

I was on my way home when I see Decky Flynn.

He saw me. Oh he lit up when he saw me. I could feel the knot in me stomach. Go on, just get on with it, you prick. Call me a name. Go on, do your worst.

He kicks a football over at me. It hits me in the shin then deflects back towards him. He's stalking me now. He's the lion: the head of the pack. All the lads not far behind now: about five of them. All grinning, licking their lips. If I wasn't so threatened, I'd have found it quite homoerotic. But that's me. So up he comes.

"Why didn't you kick the ball back, Bobby?"

I said nothing and kept walking. Decky had this aura about him that was intimidating. As I kept walking, I felt a football connect with the back of my head and I lost me footing. Decky was baring down on me like a grizzly bear. Sneering and laughing.

***

BOBBY: There's your fucking ball.

DECKY: Who do you think you're talking to? Were you trying to kick the ball up to your oul wan? Sure, she won't catch it.

***

When I get home. The house is empty. Dad's in work. Again. I clean meself up and I start to cry again. And the tears are flowing faster than the blood that poured from my nose.

I put on Madonna. The *Something to Remember* album.

I start to put on some make up. And then I stop. Just as *This Used to Be My Playground* is playing.

What am I thinking? That the world is gonna change because I throw on a pair of heels and some lipstick? The world will just tell me what I am. Decky Flynn will tell me what I am.

Queer. And all the rest.

That that is all I'll ever be.

10. KAREN – Karen versus Bernie

Bobby said to me once, "They say it's brave; don't they?"

To come out!

Why should it be brave just to exist as your true self?

Because people hate what they don't understand. And sometimes, there's just no black and white. Which is ironic. Just hatred. Pure and simple hatred and ignorance. And some people won't ever change. Like Bernie Flynn. And her spawn, Decky.

I banged down her door the night her little bollix attacked Bobby. I had to drag it out of Bobby. The mark left on the side of his face. He was in an awful state. I rang Mandy. She came straight up to the house. Well, I marched up to that house like a woman possessed. Not my flesh and blood, let me tell you. Never.

I saw the bitch. She wouldn't answer the door. I saw her in the window. She wouldn't budge. I roared through the letterbox –

> "Bernie, your yunfella is after giving my nephew a
> hiding. Open the door. I want a word."

I nearly broke the letterbox. Let me tell you, I've a temper when I get going. You don't cross me. You don't ever cross me.

All the neighbours on her street gawping. And I had no problem telling them all what her Decky did. Mandy's mother followed me up to the house. Imelda. A timid little woman with a heart of gold.

*"Karen, I'm telling you now, get back down to that
house. You'll end up getting arrested. She's not worth
it."*

Oh, I would have been arrested. I would have knocked the head off
her and I'm only waiting to see that little shit of hers.

Mick was having none of it, of course. Bobby went quiet. Wouldn't
talk up. Mick telling him it's only a bit of jeering. Lads being lads.
He rang Bernie. She said she'd get a Mass said for our Angie. Oh I
went spare. I went fucking apeshit. I had war with Mick.

He hurled the same insults back. Waster this, get a job that. Rinse
and repeat.

*"You're lucky you're Angie's sister and Bobby's
godmother. Cos if you weren't, you wouldn't set foot
in my house."*

I went to the pub. I drank everything. Shorts for most of the night.
Then I met Sandra Halpin. And we bitched about Bernie Flynn.
Bernie got Sandra sacked from the hairdressers. Accused her of
damaging her hair and threatened to sue the salon. She spread it
around the whole town. She wanted to have Mandy done for assault
once. Poor Imelda, crying up in me face. Thinking Mandy was
gonna end up on *Prisoner: Cell Block H* cos she kicked Decky in
the balls.

I came out of the chipper with Sandra at 2 am that night. And I had
a bottle of Smirnoff in me handbag. We walked up to Bernie's
house. No doubt, she was dead to the world, in the bed with Tony.
An out-and-out dickhead is Tony Flynn. Always out canvassing for
Fianna Fáil. And coaching the kids' hurling teams. Never lifted a
hurley in his life. The only thing he ever lifted was a couple of
Rolex watches from a shop in town years ago. Oh, he denied it. But

mud sticks. Shifty little man. Meant to have played away a few times as well.

And Bernie. When she's not up in the church, she's on the sunbed. Yeah, she gives out Communion out in the church. She's like Hulk Hogan going around. Always in red and yellow. I get a migraine looking at her, never mind listening to her. I'd do time for her. She's like a cross between Hyacinth Bucket from *Keeping Up Appearances* and Mrs Slocombe from *Are You Being Served?*.

She turns her nose up at everyone.

I wouldn't mind, she came from nothing. Her mother, Betty, would have robbed the eye out of your head. And her brother, Frankie. Well they used to call him The Fist Flynn. He had more fights than Mohammed Ali.

He's a born-again Christian now. Always handing out leaflets in town bout the rapture. The rapture? Wasn't that something Debbie Harry sang?

Just before we got to the House of Flynn. I took the key to my flat and very carefully walked up to Bernie's little Fiat Punto. And I scratched the door and to be honest, I enjoyed every minute of it. Within seconds, her car alarm went off. And meself and Sandra saw a light go on in the house.

And part of me wanted to stay there. Let her pull up the blind and see me outside her house. And blow her a kiss that would transition into a middle finger.

I did something worse that night. I walked all the way up to the graveyard. Four am in the morning. Thankfully, it was bright. And I sat at Angie's grave. And I blacked out.

I was looking out for me godchild that night. And still looking out for me sister.

11. BOBBY – At My Mother's Heels

I'm not a tranny. That's what my father says about drag queens. Thinks they're all trannies. But I've caught him watching Lily Savage and Dame Edna. He do be pissing himself. Karen knows a drag queen in London. She's called Connie Lingus. She plays in this place called The Vauxhall Tavern. His real name's Emmet.

Karen bought me my first pair of heels. I used to rob me mother's. I've kept all her good shoes. Mam actually caught me once. In her heels. I was just messing around. She just burst out laughing and said, "Get them off ya, for fuck sake. I have that dinner dance on Saturday night. Go out and play."

I wish I was more like Mandy. She doesn't give a shit. Mandy has an energy when she walks into a room. I shrink.

I don't fit in. I just don't. And I feel it more the past year with Mam gone. I don't fit. Bobby Burke doesn't fit. Maybe I will someday.

When I'm dressed up. And performing. It's like I can hide behind the make-up and the wigs. The heels. Dancing around. I'm someone else for a few minutes. I'm somebody. Cos you'd be sick of being nobody. And feeling like you're nobody.

It's freedom. Pure and simple. Freedom from myself. Shy, awkward, Bobby Burke. Freedom from the endless names that fall like rain. Freedom!!!

That I do fit. It's like a suit of armour.

"Express yourself, don't repress yourself" –
Madonna on *Human Nature* from *Bedtime Stories*,
1994.

Freedom to express myself. To be strong. In my own skin. To be a shiny, pretty thing in a material, mixed up, fucked-up world.

Drag doesn't judge. It doesn't care where you're from, or who you sleep with. It's living out loud, in full-on colour. It's looking like an absolute star. Cos everyone's a star after midnight. Drag is sport for gay people. And I'm playing ball.

And in the dark of night, the world is a cold, hard place. And drag colours it. It brightens it. It screams under disco balls and dances till dawn and demands to be heard. And I, Bobby Burke, demand to be seen and heard.

There's a talent competition in the City Theatre.

I'm back in school the following Wednesday.

Mandy thinks I should do it. So does Karen.

'I dare ya. I absolutely dare ya.'

12. MANDY – Buggy Spice

I took another two pregnancy tests. They were both positive. I've been numb ever since. Panicking, crying, thinking the worst possible case scenario.

I thought, surely there was some mistake. That the tests were faulty. Decky rang me. I'd been avoiding him all week. Been avoiding everyone actually. Bobby was ringing constantly about outfits for the talent show. I just wanted to hide away from the world.

I agreed to meet Decky. I don't know why. Part of me thought he might suss me out. But then again, Decky is as thick as shit at the best of times.

I met him anyway. Lied to Bobby. Again. That was becoming a bit of a habit as the summer went on.

Decky was waiting for me at a bench in the park. It was a gorgeous July evening. Felt like the whole town was out. I felt uneasy in myself. Distant. Detached. Funnily enough, how I normally feel when I get me period.

I kissed him. He stank of curry and Tayto salt and vinegar. I looked at him. And I mean I really looked.

My god! This fucking eejet had managed to get me pregnant. I felt physically sick.

He kept trying to hand me a naggin. I told him I was on antibiotics and couldn't drink.

So he knocked it back and did his usual. Decky had this toxic trait of slagging everybody and anybody off.

Of course, there was the usual bile about Bobby. I stopped him in his tracks. But he could see he was winding me up, and so I let it go. Didn't want to give him the satisfaction. He loved that, did Decky. Feeding on knowing he was winding people up.

As we sat there, a girl who was in our school walked past pushing a buggy. It was Becky Hanlon. Becky was 15 when she got pregnant. She dropped out of school. I remember how it was seen as some sort of scandal around the place. But here she was, at 17, with the cutest little boy in her buggy.

I thought I was looking at my future. She gave me a nod of acknowledgment as she walked past. It was almost as if she knew. Like she was passing the baton for single teen mothers onto me.

Decky then let out a deafening roar –

"Look at fucking Buggy Spice!"

My blood went cold.

"Buggy Spice!"

Becky kept walking and ignored him.

I couldn't though. I got up off the bench and walked off.

"Where are you going?" he bellows.

"Wherever you're not."

And I kept walking. Until I was running. And then crying. I stopped meeting Decky after that.

Buggy Spice!!!

What a prick.

So, Decky started seeing someone else. Some girl called Louise. Louise the Sleaze. He ignored me for ages. Then, randomly declares he's with this girl. I called him every name under the sun. He called me a slut. And told me to fuck off and play with the queer. I told him to fuck off and play with his mother. And told him he was riddled. He probably is too. He can't even tie his own shoelaces, let alone unwrap a Johnnie.

Oh, he's in the talent show. He has a band. They're called Slide Away. They do dodgy covers of Oasis and Nirvana. They are absolutely beyond shit. He's the lead singer. He hasn't a note in his head. Dickhead.

That show is four weeks away. Summer moves on fast. When you get your summer holidays, you think you have forever and a day to piss around and do nothing. Then, before you know, you're back in school.

I hate school. I'm not a fool. I get good reports. I pass everything. I'm a cheeky bitch. I've a smart mouth. I answer back. Course, you can't do that in school. My favourite thing about school is having a sneaky fag whilst Bobby goes white in the face every time he hears a footstep. He'd be reading *Hello Magazine* while I puff away. Were both obsessed with Princess Diana. Like I hate the Royal Family. They started the Famine, according to Bobby. But I love Princess Di. I hope she marries that Dodi fella. Bobby is dressing up as Princess Diana this Halloween.

I daydream out the window half the time. I don't wanna stay in this town. Nothing ever happens in this town.

I don't want to go to college. Spend another four years in books? And for what?

A scroll to tell me I can sit in the same job till I'm in me 60s? No thanks.

Students are wankers anyway. I wanna save up and run. Anywhere bar here.

I nearly told Bobby tonight. That I was pregnant. I need to tell someone before I explode.

I was so close to opening me mouth. He noticed as well.

> *"Mandy, what's wrong with you? You're so quiet*
> *tonight."*

I lied and told him I was getting me period. If only. Oh sure, he freaked out. I told him to chill out. You'd swear he was gonna catch menstruation off me.

13. DECKY – A Mother's Love

The Mr Whippy ice-cream van used to always spin around our estate at 7pm in the evening.

We used to always chase it and throw stones at the back of it. Your man who drove it stopped the van one night and chased a gang of us.

Whippy drives up. And stares daggers at me. I throw him the finger and he starts ranting and raving out the window. We all just started laughing and … the fucking eejet.

Then, one of the lads ran over.

"Did you hear???"

"Angie Burke is dead."

At first, the name didn't ring a bell. And then he followed it up with –

"Bobby Burke's mother in our class. His mother is after dying."

There was a silence amongst us all.

I looked over and I could see me own mother crying. And then she was walking towards me. Dabbing her eyes.

"Is it true?" I said.

"Is what true?"

"That Bobby Burke's mam is after dying."

*"Yeah, love. It is. Bed of heaven to the poor woman.
Get into the house. I need you to babysit your little
brother for an hour. I'm going down to Mass."*

The day of Bobby Burke's mother's funeral, me mother made me wait outside the church and pay my respects.

I hate stuff like that. Stuff like funerals. It scares me. The whole town seemed to come to a standstill.

I felt more and more uneasy the closer the procession came to the church.

And then I saw the coffin.

***

DECKY: Mandy.

MANDY: What do ya want?

Any more names for me?

DECKY: What are you on about?

MANDY: Randy Mandy.

Not ring a bell, no?

And I thought my mouth was big.

Don't you dare talk about me like that, you ignorant prick.

Now piss off and leave me alone before I throw those chips all over you.

DECKY: I'm sorry, Mandy.

MANDY: Sure you are.

Fellas like you are never sorry.

DECKY: Do you want a chip?

Are you alright?

MANDY: Doesn't matter.

DECKY: It does.

Does to me.

Mandy stares at Decky momentarily.

Are you alright?

MANDY: No.

I'm not alright.

My best friend's mother laid out in a coffin.

I was mad about that woman.

MANDY: I have to go.

I have to call up to Bobby. I don't want him on his own.

I just needed to get out of there for a while. Was a bit much.

Mandy is now on her feet and braced to go.

DECKY: Mandy.

MANDY: Yeah?

DECKY: Can I ring you?

I'll ring you.

MANDY: If you want.

DECKY: Okay.

I'm around.

MANDY: Decky?

DECKY: Yeah?

MANDY: Nothing.

It's grand. Doesn't matter.

I better go.

See ya later.

DECKY: See ya, Mandy.

14. KAREN – Empty Bottles and White Feathers

I think they call it self-medicating. That's the new trendy and hip 90s expression. I drink. I'm harming no one.

"You're harming yourself," says Mick. Like he's fucking Oprah.

I'm harmed years. Harmed and haunted.

I gave Angie her first drink. We were on holiday with our parents. Me father had a caravan in Courtown. And he'd hide drink in a little press. Whiskey was his poison. Me mother liked a gin and tonic.

Himself and me mother were asleep on one side of the caravan. And me and Angie were still up. I snuck down and pulled out a bottle of Blue Nun. And we went outside in our dressing gowns and sat on this mound of grass and drank the thing dry. We went to bed after we had downed it. Next thing I know, she was puking up all over the caravan. It was carnage. The mother and father straight up out of bed. Me mother slipped on the vomit and brought down a pile of plates that smashed off the ground. I dragged Angie out of the caravan, held back her hair until she got it all up. And little did I know, on that summer's night, I'd be doing the same almost twenty years later. Only it was the chemo making her vomit.

There was one night I wiped her down and she was almost hysterical. Sweating. She was in pain. I was putting another basin beside her bed. And she stopped me dead. Stared at me.

"It's only a bit of sick, Angie," I said.

And she started crying.

I got up beside her and put me arm around her. I choked back the lump. It was as big as a boulder in me throat. Don't cry, Karen. You're the big sister. Not now. Hold it in now. Cry in your own time. Not in front of her.

"Karen, will you do me a favour?"

And the pause was longer than the night.

"When I go, Karen, will you make sure Bobby is looked after? Will you do that for me? I never ask you for anything. But I'm asking you now. Will you make sure me baby boy is looked after? Cos I won't be here."

And she broke down. And I broke down worse. Like a house of cards, I folded. I wanted to scream into the dark.

"You're not going anywhere. Okay. You're not going anywhere."

She was dead a month later.

No amount of alcohol will purge the memories of those last moments. My god, Mick. He was so strong that night. But he was in another world.

I climbed up on the bed and lay in beside her. And I could hear how shallow her breathing was.

And I clutched the Medjugorje medal me mother gave me. And I looked up to the sky and I said, "God, I'm begging you, for that child, for my Bobby, will you please spare me sister? I'm on me knees. Please god, I'm begging you. Make it go away. Make it go away. Give it to me."

And I started singing *Edelweiss* from *The Sound Of Music*. That was our favourite film as kids.

And as the night went on, the breathing was just a hum. Me on one side of her and Mick on the other.

And all I remember her saying was,

> *"The angels!!! I can see them. The angels are coming for me."*

And they came. And she left. My angel. My baby sister.

> *"The angels are coming for me."*

I hear it on a loop the last 12 months. It plays on repeat, in widescreen technicolour. At the end of each wine glass, wine bottle, empty can and empty pint glass.

That memory.

Waking up amongst empty bottles. Empty bottles and white feathers.

White feathers. My mother always said, "When you see a white feather, it means a loved one is near."

White feathers.

Empty bottles and white feathers.

15. MICK – Confessions at a Graveyard

Things are getting to me a bit lately. Angie's anniversary is looming. My head is all over the place. And I know I'm working too much. But when I'm busy, me mind doesn't wander. Doesn't overthink. It's all coming back to me lately. A year without Angie.

And then I get wind of this talent competition. Thinking he might get up and sing. He wants to be a drag queen. A drag queen!! He'll be the talk of the town. I heard it from Karen. I caught her with some consent form and his name on it. And her signature. And my forged signature. I said to her, "What's that in your handbag?".

I thought she was on the fiddle. And then, out it all came. I don't need this. And she lecturing me. Her lecturing me.

"Ah wake up, Mick. You're living in that factory.
Surely, you know Bobby is more Quentin Crisp than
Quentin Tarantino."

Well I lost the head.

"We can't all spend our dole being a barfly and easy
lay around the town. You had your sister's heart
broken. Lecturing me on my son, when you got rid of
your own."

She went white. I shouldn't have said it. I could almost see Angie standing there, looking disgusted. There was silence. I'm not a cruel man. She was on the edge of tears and she stormed out of the house.

I sat down for the night. Put on all the old records me and Angie would listen to. All I wanted to see was Bobby. Talk him out of doing something stupid. Having the whole place talk about him. Time I stepped up. Steered him right. He's not right for that life. He's 16. What the hell do you know at 16? I waited up for him. I was watching *TFI Friday*. Me usual Friday night routine. Had a few cans.

He walked into the sitting room. I could smell the drink off him. And to be honest, I was relieved. I felt he was being a normal teenager. But it's 1997 and I don't know what normal is anymore. Maybe I don't want to know. Angie was better with these things. Karen is better at these things. He sat down on the settee.

"What's all this about?"

"All what about?" he says.

"You dressing up."

"It's drag."

I got up off the chair and I paced the sitting room. Be calm, Mick. For the love of God.

"I'm protecting you, Bobby. You're 16."

"Protecting me from what?"

"From what the whole place will call you."

"They call me every name under the sun as it is."

*"Don't give them an excuse to call you anymore.
Why don't you come to me? I'm your father."*

And he got up and he roared.

> *"You're never here!!!! You're never here, dad. You don't listen. Mammy listened. Karen listens. Mandy listens. You never listen."*

And it cut like a knife.

> *"I'm listening now. Life is hard enough as it is. I don't want you making it any harder for yourself."*

> *"I've lost me mam. How much harder can it get?"*

> *"We can talk to someone."*

> *"I'M TALKING TO YOU!!!!"*

> *"It's drag, dad. You don't have to understand it. It's freedom I don't have in a school unform. It's hard to explain. Its like a suit of armour. But underneath it all, it's all me. Every little bit. I can't just switch off who I wanna be. And I can't just switch off who I am."*

I said, "Look, we will figure this out."

> *"There's nothing to figure out. I'm going to bed."*

And I grabbed him. And I held him with all my might. As tight as when the midwife presented him to me on that stormy November night in 1980.

I went up to Angie's grave the next morning. I had a restless night. Bobby was still in bed. I looked in on him. He snoring his head off in the bed. Surrounded by a pile of *Smash Hits* magazines. And Pepsi wrappers. Princess Diana beside him on the press. His guinea pig.

I got up to the grave. And I lay down flowers. And I break down to her.

> *"I've messed up, girl. I've messed up. You said it years. I was a stubborn fucker. You were right. You were always right. I've fucked up, Angie. I've fucked up. I took me eye off the ball with Bobby. I'm trying. Believe me, I'm trying. You were always better at this stuff. I should be protecting him, Angie. I am. I am.*

> *"It's been hard, Angie. Too hard. Too cruel. I thought when you went, the world would stop being so cold and cruel. They never said it'd be this cruel."*

And little did I know, Bobby was standing behind me. He put his hand on my shoulder.

> *"I just wanted to give Mam these. Dad, you don't need to protect me. What would you think mam would say if she was here?"*

I didn't hesitate.

> *"Honestly, Bobby. Your mother would tell you to do whatever makes you happy."*

He paused for a moment and sat down.

> *"Dad, you know I'm different."*

> *"You're no different than anyone else."*

"Look, I know you think I'm too young to know me
own mind. And I feel like anything I say, you'll just
think its linked to Mam not being here. And I get
that; I really do.

"But you need to know something. And I didn't think
this would be the place I'd be telling you this ...

"I'm gay."

And I could see something change in him the minute he said it. And
in me too, I suppose. In a good way. I knew. Sure, I always knew.

"I'm proud of you," I said. "And so is your mam.
And your aunty. But I'm prouder than the two of
them put together. Me and you against the world, kid.
Always.

***

Mick is laying down flowers, unaware that Bobby is
overhearing his conversation with Angie's headstone.

MICK: I've messed up, girl. I've messed up. You've said it
yourself years. I was a stubborn fucker. You were always right.

I've messed up Angie. God forgive me, I've fucked up. I took me
eye off the ball with Bobby. I'm trying. Believe me, I'm trying.

You always said, "God loves a tryer."

I don't know, maybe he's gone off me. Maybe I stopped believing.

You were always better at this stuff. I'm trying to protect him,
Angie.

I am. I really am.

It's been hard. Too cruel. I thought when you left, the world would stop being so cold and cruel.

Never thought it'd be this cruel.

BOBBY: I just wanted to give Mam these.

Bobby is clutching flowers

Dad, you don't need to protect me.

MICK: Bobby, what's all this about?

You dressing up?

BOBBY: It's drag.

MICK: I'm just trying to protect you.

You're 16.

BOBBY: From what?

MICK: From what people will call you.

BOBBY: They call me every name under the sun as it is. What's a few more?

You could publish an encyclopaedia with the words I've been called.

MICK: Well, don't give them an excuse to call you anymore.

Why don't you come to me.

I'm your father.

> *Bobby will become angry at this point and roar the next line.*

BOBBY: YOU'RE NEVER HERE!!!!!!!

You're never here, Dad. You don't listen. Mam listened. Karen listens. Mandy listens.

You never listen.

Mick grabs Bobby by the shoulders.

MICK: I'm listening now. Life is hard enough as it is. I don't want you making it any harder for yourself.

BOBBY: I've lost me mam.

How much harder can it get?

MICK: We can talk to someone.

BOBBY: I'M TALKING TO YOU!

It's drag, dad. You don't have to understand it.

It's freedom. Freedom. I don't have in a school uniform.

It's hard to explain. It's like a suit of armour. But underneath it. It's all me. Every little bit.

And yeah, maybe it sounds like I'm talking utter bollocks.

But I can't switch off who I wanna be.

And I can't just switch off who I am.

Begins to sob.

I can't. I just can't.

I'm different.

MICK: You're no different than anyone else.

BOBBY: I'm gay, Dad.

Mick pulls Bobby into his chest for a long and emotional embrace. Bobby is overcome with emotion.

MICK: You're okay.

I'm proud of you.

And so is your mam.

Me and you against the world, kid.

Karen enters the scene

KAREN: A drag queen.

Jesus Bobby, I thought you were gonna get a trade.

Are you alright yeah?

BOBBY: Ask me in an hour.

Are you alright?

KAREN: I'll be alright once I stop doing this to myself.

I'm too old for this shit. Way past too old. This is not living. It's not worth it.

Living an endless cycle of hangovers, barflies and bad karaoke.

What am I doing to myself? Is it self-medicating or is it punishment?

Because she's lying under that headstone.

I can't carry on living like this. Can't keep doing the 'I'll start tomorrow' or 'I'll start next week'.

I just need to start.

BOBBY: Come on. We'll head to the beach.

They're giving it good till the weekend.

Karen, are you coming?

KAREN: Mick, will you gimme a minute?

I'll follow the pair of you out to the carpark.

Just need a minute.

MICK: You know where we are.

KAREN: Mick.

MICK: Yeah?

KAREN: Thanks.

> *Scene ends with Karen on stage smiling at Angie's headstone as Edelweiss begins to play.*

16. KAREN – The Last Hangover

I woke up in Mick and Angie's spare room. And immediately my head was stuck in another vomit-soaked basin. Angie's Mass card looking up at me from the carpet.

I can't keep doing this to myself. I can't. I'm too old for this shit. I'm way past too old. This is not living. It's not. This is not worth it.

I'm heading into me early 40s. And my life is an endless cycle of hangovers, horny barflies, vomit and bad karaoke.

What am I doing to myself? Is it self-medicating or is it punishment? Because Angie died? Because I had an abortion at 17? I don't know. And the little I do know is that I can't carry on living like this. Can't keep doing the 'I'll start tomorrow' or 'I'll start next week'.

I just need to start.

Start living. Cos this isn't living.

17. MANDY – The Mixtape

I can't sleep. The heat is stifling. And my mind is racing. I'm still with child. For now. I'm not keeping it. God, I hope he wins. He deserves it. His outfit. Mam IS just putting the finishing touches on it.

I made him a mixtape. I always make mixtapes when I can't sleep. Or if my mind is racing over stuff. I rang some helpline the other night. And then I hung up. I was embarrassed. But also, I know my own mind. A mind that's been racing since those two blue lines appeared on that test.

As for Decky. The doting father to be. Well, if my mind was made up, he sealed the deal. Word on the street is he's with every girl in the town. More fool them. And more fool me. I couldn't imagine him as a father.

I've put ten songs on it. Stuff he has anyway and some just to annoy him. Like Alanis Morrisette. I put *Ironic* on it, cos he hates that song. He says its not one bit ironic.

I put some Madonna on. Then some Spice Girls. That new girlband, All Saints. *Freed from Desire* by Gala. That's been our summer anthem.

Bittersweet Symphony by The Verve. Cos sometimes I feel like Richard Ashcroft in that video. I just wanna walk down the street and shoulder every fucker out of my way.

I got him a good luck card.

And before I tried to sleep, I wrote on Bobby's card –

"To Bobby, my material boy, you're gonna blow the roof off the place. Love, your best friend, xx Mandy.

"P.S: Can you keep a secret? I'm pregnant. – Mandy."

18. BOBBY/MICK/KAREN – The Bitch Rang the Radio

BOBBY: I did it. I told my father I'm gay. The world didn't fall in. The jukebox in the Queen Vic didn't stop. Things feel better at home. Never in a million years did I think I'd come out to him at me mother's graveside.

I still don't think he's on board with the drag thing though. I haven't pressed it. I've just let it be. I feel being gay was enough for him to digest. Before he sees me in full costume.

Mandy's mother is gonna sew my costume. She said we could have a fitting in her kitchen.

I've been practising. So not just Madonna, but mostly Madonna. I still have time to tell them what track I wanna do.

I'm trying to narrow it down.

I was in Mandy's this morning. We said we'd have a run through. I was happy in myself. After the past year, I've felt myself settle. Even me father. Like it's still hard. Without mam. As the summer goes on, I don't know, there feels some kind of shift. Like I know me life will never be the same again. But there seemed to be a calming. It was like myself, dad and Karen. We got through the longest night.

And the sun was starting to sneak through the clouds.

And then …

THE BITCH RANG THE RADIO!

***

MICK: I'm on days this week. 6 to 2. Suited me, that shift. Could bring Bobby off for a spin after I got home from work.

We always have ChatFM on in the factory. Your man, Barry, who hosts the morning show. He has every Tom, Dick and Harry ring in every morning. And all they do is moan and complain. But he plays good music. Always plays a request for me and the lads on Line 4.

So I get back to work after a quick cup of tea and chat with Tab Anderson, me line manager. And I'm doing me usual routine.

The Premiership was nearly back. The usual slagging between Liverpool and Man United fans. United had signed Sheringham and Paul Ince had jumped enemy lines to Anfield. And all the talk was about Arsenal.

So the radio is blaring and on comes Barry. A bitta Texas, the new Oasis single lined up, a bitta Aslan.

And next thing, its only Bernie Flynn. And she's giving out. She's giving out about my son.

THE BITCH ONLY RANG THE FUCKING RADIO!

***

KAREN: So I'm nursing a headache And I do me usual. Two paracetamol and ChatFM. I love Barry's show. He gets some lunatics ringing in. He had a woman ring in last week saying there was an ink mark on her credit union book that resembled St Theresa of the Roses. Barry sent her out a Tesco voucher.

So I sit down and turn the dial and next thing I hear is Bernie Flynn.

THE BITCH ONLY RANG THE FUCKING RADIO!

19. Radio Scene

BARRY: That was Ultra Nate and *Free* on ChatFM. A huge hit in Ibiza this summer. Phone lines are open and music still to come this hour from The Verve, Boyzone and that brand new Oasis single ahead of *Be Here Now*, out on August 21st.

Good morning, Bernie.

BERNIE: Good morning, Barry.

BARRY: Bernie, what do you want to chat about this morning?

BERNIE: Well, Barry, I want to talk about the talent show in the City Theatre in August.

As a mother, I have some concerns.

BARRY: Concerns, Bernie? Do tell us more.

BERNIE: Barry, it is my belief that a young drag queen will be one of the acts taking part. Now Barry, I don't think that kind of act is appropriate. And I think it sets a very dangerous precedent. Especially with a family audience. An impressionable audience being exposed to this sort of vulgarity. Its not right to normalise something that, let's be honest, Barry, is not normal.

BARRY: But Bernie, drag has been around for decades.

BERNIE: Now hang on, Barry. An act that young performing as a crossdresser promotes a lifestyle that is questionable. A lifestyle, Barry, that is not normal. It is vulgar and perverse and against everything that is written in the Bible. And that lifestyle is homosexuality.

BARRY: Now Bernie, I'd suggest you be careful, please.

BERNIE: Barry, I don't beat around the bush. This is a talent competition, showcasing the youth in this city. This is not Amsterdam. I'm actually appalled that a kid so young would opt to dress like a transvestite and wiggle around like a Spice Girl. Or Mr Pussy. A bitta common sense and cop on wouldn't go amiss.

BARRY: Bernie, I have someone on the line who wants to come in on this. Good morning, Karen.

KAREN: Good morning, Barry.

BARRY: Have you a response to Bernie?

KAREN: Who the hell are you to come on the radio and target a kid? And rant about what's normal? I don't care what the Bible says. Who are you trying to kid?

Sure, the only thing you read is the *Argos* catalogue.

BERNIE: Excuse me!

KAREN: I'll excuse nothing, Bernie. People like you and your beloved Church holding back this country decades. Do as I say and not as I do. Hiding behind quotes and hypocrisy. But you keep praying. Say a novena to St Antony and see if he can find you a bit of cop on for yourself.

BERNIE: Maybe you should pray to him.

KAREN: Oh, I will. I'll ask him to find me an extra fuck to give.

BARRY: Karen, I won't accept that language.

BERNIE: It's not normal.

KAREN: What's not normal is a woman in her 50s …

BERNIE: I'm actually 42.

KAREN: Like fuck you are. And I'm Pamela Anderson.

BARRY: We'll have no swearing. This is a live broadcast.

KAREN: You're more than welcome to your beliefs, Bernie, but there is certainly nothing perverse about drag queens.

And furthermore, when you're done polishing St Antony's balls up in the church …

BERNIE: I'm an educated woman. I have a degree.

KAREN: In what, Bernie? Fuckology?

BARRY: Hang on now, Karen, less of the swearing.

KAREN: Your beliefs don't give you the right to belittle anyone for who they are. And certainly not my nephew, or any other gay person in this city.

BERNIE: Well, you're certainly no role model to him. That's for sure.

KAREN: And you're no spring chicken. Ain't nobody gonna suddenly turn gay because of a drag queen. And you lecturing on what's normal, like some spokeswoman for the Vatican. Funny, Bernie, how there wasn't a peep out of you when Barry covered clerical abuse. Did you pipe up then?

No, but you'll happily target a kid and spout shit on the radio.

BARRY: We'll have no shit please, Karen.

KAREN: Ask her about her own kid, Barry. Bullying half the town.

BERNIE: My yunfella is on the county team.

KAREN: I couldn't care less if he's on *Gladiators*.

BERNIE: Well it's a more normal outlet than dressing like Mr Pussy.

KAREN: Well, you're no Princess Diana yourself, Bernie. And by Christ, he looks better in drag than you do when you're handing out Communion.

Bernie, who does your make up? Stevie Wonder?

BARRY: Okay ladies, we will leave it there.

BERNIE: You don't get to defame my son on the radio. My family are very well respected in this community. And through my husband's campaigning with Fianna Fáil, we have contributed very positively to this city. And your social welfare allowance.

KAREN: Ah go on, ring Bertie. Tell him I'm still waiting on that extension he promised me when he banged down me door with your husband.

BARRY: We're gonna have to cut it there, ladies.

KAREN: The neck of you, Bernie. We all remember your oul wan fiddling the diddly club out in the factory. Tenerife was it, Bernie? Cos she called in sick for a fortnight with shingles, yet breezed back in two weeks later, like Cilla Black on the sunbed.

Not a morrig on her.

BARRY: Okay, we will leave it there. Thank you, Karen. Thank you, Bernie.

Now, here's music from The Beautiful South.

On ChatFM.

20. MICK – Sticks and Stones and Bernie Flynn

I've always been able to stand up for meself. Stand me ground. I was never a fella who got into fights or arguments. But I always stood me ground. Never let anyone walk all over me. This competition is creeping up. And weeks on, my blood is still boiling over Bernie Flynn on the radio.

But I've been overwhelmed by the amount of people saying he's right. The amount of people backing him. People are good like that. And it's sold out. And I keep telling Bobby, he can drop out at any time. But he's full steam ahead. And yet that woman's words still ring in me ears, like nails on a chalkboard.

She went into hiding. She let off her bomb on the radio. And herself, Tony and Decky flew off to Lanzarote for a fortnight. Alright for some. So, I get word she's back. And I decide, I'm gonna call her out. And furthermore, I'm bringing Bobby with me.

I'm about to collect him from Mandy's when I hear an almighty thud off the front door. Like a bomb had gone off. And it did. Karen. Louder than Hiroshima. Falls into the hall at lunchtime. I bite me lip for once. I don't need this, Karen. And she don't need it. And I can feel myself about to explode till I catch the picture of Angie in the corner. Like she was telling me to hold my fire.

I brought Karen up the stairs and into the spare bedroom. Put down the basin beside the bed.

"I'm sorry, Mick. I'm sorry."

And then she nodded off. And as she nodded off, she let Angie's Mass card slip from her shirt pocket. And I just studied it for a few minutes.

And as Karen lay there asleep, I just whispered –

"Minding your sister. You need to mind yourself."

I left her sleep and went and got Bobby. Poor Imelda, trying to convince me to leave it go. Mandy insisted on coming. Bobby looked terrified. I wasn't out to intimidate the woman. I was out to defend my son. Defend my family. I felt like John Wayne walking to the Alamo. Mandy marched up the road. Chewing bubble-gum and blowing bubbles. Bobby looked distant. But I wanted him there.

And then I clock her. Herself and Tony in the front garden. Sitting out on two sun loungers, like they were still in Lanzarote. Him reading *The Sun* and her leafing through *Woman's Way*. Costa Del Flynn. And then, who do I spot? Only little fists of fury himself, the elusive Decky Flynn. The great white hope of intercounty hurling. He went white when he saw me. I could see Bobby tense up when he saw him.

"Bernie," I said, with gritted teeth.

Tony looked instantly uneasy. As he should. As for her. Ice cold. Yet painting on a pretend smile.

"Can I help you?"

Decky still looked nervous. I grinned at him. The more I grinned, the more uncomfortable he looked. Mandy was staring holes through him. I'd leave him be for now than make him squirm.

I'm not a vengeful man. I don't believe in bitterness. It's a poison that drains you dry and robs you of basic joy. I've had the worst year of me life, but I'm not bitter.

"Bernie, you can help me by telling me who the hell
are you to talk about my son on the radio?"

First shot. Pistols drawn. Oh, she didn't flinch. Tony was beginning to sweat.

"I'm entitled to my opinion. I know it mustn't be easy
for the two of you after poor Angela."

"Don't even go there. You knew full well what you
were doing. And don't even mention my wife."

Tony got up.

"I think we all have our wires crossed here."

And as Tony fluttered around like a demented butterfly, I could see my Bobby just stare at her intently. His expression didn't change once. He just stared at the woman. She didn't yield.

"Spouting your bullshit on the radio like some
fishwife about my son. Like some town crier. When
him, yeah him ..."

I was staring right at Decky now.

"... when he marked my son."

Strike one. His head was down and her eyes were lit up, like the grotto she has beside her porch.

"Ah, see here now ..." piped up Tony.

Bernie cut him off.

"My Declan didn't touch him. And when you have a son behaving like that ..."

She points at Bobby at this point.

"... Let's be honest, Mr Burke, they do ask for it; don't they? Anything to be different."

"A boy in a dress. You must be so proud."

Oh she went low. I clocked Decky grinning. Keep it calm, Mick.

"I'm very proud of my son. And I'll be even prouder when he's up on that stage. In a dress."

"But are you proud, Bernie? Ringing a radio station and speaking about a 16-year-old kid like he's some sort of monster. Some sort of threat. All whilst clutching your pound-shop pearls. The model Catholic. All because you collect the basket in St Mary's of a Sunday morning."

Again, she didn't flinch. I didn't expect her to. I'm not naïve.

"I'm entitled to my beliefs."

"Oh you are, Bernie. And I'm entitled to not to give a fiddler's piss about them."

At this point, Mandy bursts out laughing.

"A bitter life you must lead."

She cuts me off here.

"I have a very good life."

And I paused with my pistol. And she paused. Tony looked like a fella waiting for his front lawn to swallow him up. Decky looked gormless. Bobby just stared.

"Bitterness. Hate. Where does it get you? Picking on kids. Cos let's face it, Bernie. They're still kids. Your Declan. My Bobby. They're just kids. Growing up. But they're still kids. Punching down on anyone or anything different. Well, you'll punch no more."

And at this point, I stare directly at Decky. And I can see he's about to piss his pathetic little pants. And yet the human side in me. The part that wants to see the good in people. I can see. I can see he's a messed-up 16-year-old like the rest of them. Terrified of Bernie.

"Hiding behind your rosary beads. Like it gives you permission. It just makes you look like a hypocrite."

"Now, I've said what I needed to say. But you utter my son's name again, or if him there lays as much as a look in his direction. A boy in a dress will the least of your concerns."

Mandy: Bobby, come on, were off.

Mandy struts off giggling

Bobby, he stays there. He stays stuck to the spot. And then he walks straight up to Bernie.

21. The Aftermath of the Radio Phone-In

MICK: Bernie, Tony.

Declan.

DECKY: Mr Burke.

MICK: Oh no need to stand on ceremony, Declan.

You can call me Mick.

Bernie, you can help me by telling me who the hell you are to speak about my son on the radio?

DECKY: She never mentioned Bobby.

KAREN: HE DIDN'T ASK YOU!

MICK: Spouting your bullshit on the radio like some demented fishwife about my son.

When him there marked him.

DECKY: I never touched him.

KAREN: And I'm Baby-fucking-Spice.

DECKY: He brings it on himself.

MANDY: Shut the fuck up, Decky.

DECKY: Anything for attention.

A boy in a dress.

Sure, whatever makes you proud.

MICK: Oh, I'm very proud.

I'll be even prouder when he's up on that stage in a dress.

Are you proud? Ringing a radio station and speaking about a 16-year-old like he's some sort of monster. Some sort of threat.

Bernie Flynn. The model Catholic.

KAREN: Ah sure that's her beliefs, Mick.

MICK: Well, I'm entitled not to give a fiddler's piss about them.

KAREN: A bitter life you must lead.

DECKY: Says yer woman falling out of every pub in the town.

Karen will charge towards Decky but will be held back by Mick.

KAREN: I won't be long putting you back in your box.

You'll see where that hurley will end up.

MICK: Bitterness. Hate. Where does it get you?

They're kids, Bernie. They might be 16. But my Bobby. And the All Star there. They're still kids.

Hiding behind those rosary beads like it gives you permission. It just makes you look like a hypocrite.

Now I've said what I've needed to say.

Mention his name or you …

Points at Decky.

DECKY: What about me?

KAREN: You look in his direction again or open your mouth. A boy in a dress will be the least of your worries. You'll be down that town handing out leaflets with your uncle, and you'll be wishing the fucking rapture was coming.

Oh and Bernie, if you're on the phone to Bertie Ahern. Tell him I'm still on the housing list.

MICK: Right, Karen, that's enough.

Come on. I've said me piece.

Mandy, Bobby, come on.

> *Bobby stays glued to the spot staring at Decky.*

> *He walks slowly up to Decky, confronts him. Pulls out a stick of lipstick and begins to apply it to his lips slowly, as Decky quivers with fear.*

BOBBY: I'm more than just a boy in a dress.

I'm Diana.

Diana Ciccone.

21. MICK'S FINAL MONOLOGUE

Angie died on July 19th. I remember it being the day the Atlanta Olympics were starting. I thought she'd turned a corner. All the treatment seemed to be working. Two months beforehand, we sat and watched United win the double.

I'm a man's man. I know I shouldn't say that. Cos it's nearly the millennium.

I think Angie knew. They were stuck like glue to each other. She spoiled him. I used to kill her for it. And that sister of hers. Karen O'Brien. She's a holy show. She'd give a headache an aneurism. See, Bobby talks to Karen. He wont talk to me. And I end up resenting her for it. But she's Angie's sister. She's Bobby's auntie. And I'd be lost without her, truth be told. She was always a drinker. But blacking out. Waking up with every quare hawk in the town. She's better than that. I never tell her that, but she is. She passed out at Angie's grave. Mascara down to her collarbone, white lilies in her fist and two naggins of vodka. And when she came round, all she kept saying to me was, "I'm only minding me sister. I'm just minding me sister."

Karen needs minding. More than she lets on.

Having to tell Bobby that Angie had died. Well, that was harder than holding her hand and watching her slip away. I got home. He was sitting in front of the telly. Watching *Top of the Pops*.

"Daddy, Oasis are on it tonight. Watch."

He was only 15. Angie was only 36. How the fuck is that right? He just cried into me arms. Me only child. The only other person I ever held as tight was Angie, when she took her last breath.

He wants to be a drag queen. I wanted him to get a trade. I'm learning as I go along. I haven't made peace with Angie's death. Or Bobby being ... well, whoever the fuck he wants to be. He's my son. And a father's love is stronger than anything. Stronger than whatever an ignorant mouth almighty like Bernie Flynn has to say.

Bobby.

Wouldn't change him for the world.

22. BOBBY'S FINAL MONOLOGUE –
Me versus the World

Mandy clasped me by the wrist. And just kept smiling at me. I felt physically sick. Bernie Flynn!! What she said. I went white. I could feel myself go weak.

A lifestyle that is questionable? I'm 16.

Promoting homosexuality? I wanna perform as a drag queen. What does she think I'm gonna do? Hand out leaflets on becoming a homo with a few stickers.

Vulgarity? Perverse? Was she calling me a pervert? Is that what she thinks I am?

The Bible??? What does the Bible have to do with drag? Did the 12 apostles do drag?

Sure, hang on, Bernie, I'll slip on a few sequins and do *Here I am Lord*. And the more she rabbited on, I thought, 'No, this ain't worth it.'

I was gonna ring the station and pull out. I just imagined me in the City Theatre. Being chased by Bernie Flynn with pitchforks and Bibles. Before Decky beats the shit out of me. Beats the gay out of me. He said that to me once. In the corridor in school once, he snarled at me –

"I'll beat the gay out of you."

And then Karen came on outta nowhere. I nearly choked. Mandy nearly swallowed her tongue with the laughing. And Karen was right. I'm just doing this to entertain people. Entertain myself. Don't care about winning. I never won anything in my life.

Mandy gave me a big hug and started rustling me hair and tickling me.

"Your Karen is some legend. She put that bitch in her box."

Perverse!!! What's perverse about entertaining people? I thought it was 1997. Not 1927.

A dangerous precedent! What does that mean?

And I cried. I did. I cried. I didn't bawl but I sobbed. Up in Mandy's face. Do you know what she said to me?

"Your mother would be proud of you."

And next thing I know, she pulls out five Pepsi wrappers.

"I was keeping them for you. You were collecting for some Spice Girls CD."

And just like that, I'd a full set of wrappers. Enough to get the limited-edition CD. And I started crying again.

"Jesus, you're very dramatic all yee", said Mandy.

"Who? Amanda?" goes Imelda.

"Gay people. God almighty. You're as dramatic."

"Relax," she goes, "I'm only taking the piss."

Apparently, being gay in Ireland was illegal until 1993. That was only four years ago.

Needless to say, the world will still be full of Bernie Flynns. And Decky Flynns. But I need to remember something else. For every Bernie Flynn, there's a Karen O'Brien. And for every Decky Flynn, there's a Mandy Brophy.

And then there's people like me. Bobby Burke. And we can take on the world together.

Me versus the world. In heels and sequins, with a pair of legs that won't quit.

See these.

They're still a bastard to walk in.

But don't they look absolutely fab?

Bank Lane, situated in the heart of Waterford's historic Viking triangle, will play host to *Dress You Up* for four consecutive nights in October 2024

Since launching in 2023, it has become a staple venue for live music, top comedy, theatre and all forms of entertainment and live performance.

A variety and entertainment hub that plays host to packed houses for its comedy shows. These shows have been headlined by the cream of Irish comedy, including Dylan Moran, Tony Kelly and David McSavage.

Future headliners include a host of top Irish talent including Pillow Queens, Villagers and Roisin O

For more details, please visit **BankLane.ie**

Also by Wayne Power

Everyone's a Star after Midnight

The definition of insanity is sometimes given as doing the same thing over and over again and expecting different results each time. Yet, some lessons need to be learned the hard way if understanding of the full depth of the human predicament is to be properly distilled.

Tales from the urban jungle, from Love's lost and found, of midnight masquerades and a soul laid bare. These are among the travails and adventures of the heart that await the reader in this warm and engaging collection of poems, that are passionate and intense yet deriving a solemnity that comes from learning about life's ups and downs, the high and the lows, what they have to offer us and what they tell us about ourselves.

These poems flow thick and fast but leave a lasting impression. The impact is immediate but not without surprises as the reader is taken to many places, including some that you might rather forget but others that will evoke a sense of reminiscence, maybe even make you wish that you were there.

"Love is underrated. Fear is overrated. I didn't dream it."

Published in Ireland, under the imprint of
The Manuscript Publisher, 2020. ISBN: 978-1-911442-25-7.

Available to buy online in print and e-book editions. For further information, please visit:

www.TMPpublications.com

Neon Hearts and the Angry Mob

Love in a time of lockdowns is among the themes emanating from this latest volume of poetry from Wayne Power – a worthy follow-up to his debut collection, *Everyone's a Star after Midnight*, published in 2020.

Moreover, these poems go to the very essence of love, seeing it in terms of matters that concern both the heart and the mind. It is a love that is rooted in the communities to which we belong: those that we are born into and those that we seek out (often, in search of refuge, maybe).

Written in the author's inimitable, racy style – reflecting the spoken-word, performance art that is his craft – these stories offer snapshots of the light and shade of city life, recollections of lost nights, love, mental health, also addressing social and political themes.

This is poetry at its unfiltered best, at times gritty but delivered with an unrivalled comedic edge, nourished by a sentiment steeped in fondness for where he is from, where he has been and where he hopes to go in life.

We cannot have the good without the bad, so take time to enjoy all that the world has to offer, see both sides, enjoy the things that existence reveals or has yet to tell us about ourselves and the human condition.

Published in Ireland, under the imprint of
The Manuscript Publisher, 2022. ISBN: 978-1-911442-35-6.

Available to buy online in print and e-book editions. For further information, please visit:

www.TMPpublications.com

Only When I'm Dancing Can I Feel This Free

Wayne Power's third collection of poetry contains what is arguably his strongest body of work to date, which is saying something because his previous publications – *Everyone's a Star after Midnight* from 2020 and *Neon Hearts and the Angry Mob* (2022) – were no mean feats either, that did not come up short, well received by audiences and critics alike.

Much of the terrain that his readers will be familiar with is covered here but new treasures are unearthed, on paths that might appear to be well trod, as fresh light is cast on our daily lives, our comings and our goings, where we all are at this stage in the 21st century, all conveyed in the author's inimitable racy style and unrivalled comedic edge.

"I hope people find whatever they need to find in these poems. They come from a rebel heart. A neon heart. They are the hopes, fears, unrequited feelings, the human condition, the love unspoken and said, the friendships, the kinship, the eternal family, the great beyond. They are lessons learnt. Turn your lessons into your legacy." – **Wayne Power**

Wayne Power is a writer who "speaks for and to a lot of his generation" in the words of playwright and fellow Waterford man, Jim Nolan.

Published in Ireland under the imprint of The Manuscript Publisher, 2024. ISBN: 978-1-911442-45-5 (hardcover) and 978-1-911442-44-8 (paperback)

Available to buy online in print and e-book editions. For further information, please visit:

www.TMPpublications.com